Dot to Dot
in the Sky

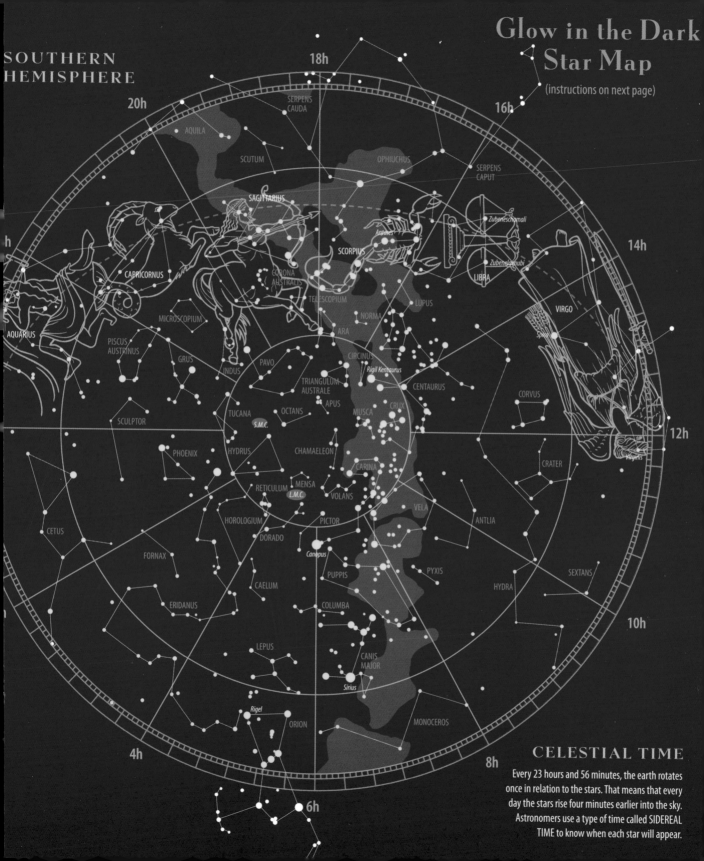

Other books by Joan Marie Galat include:

Dot to Dot in the Sky: Stories in the Stars

Dot to Dot in the Sky: Stories of the Planets

Dot to Dot in the Sky: Stories of the Moon—winner of the R. Ross Annett Children's Literature Award

Dr. Bufflehead Explores Energy (Scholastic Canada, Literacy Place for the Early Years)

Dr. Bufflehead Explores Dirt (Scholastic Canada, Literacy Place for the Early Years)

HOW TO USE THE GLOW-IN-THE-DARK STAR MAP (previous pages):
To make the stars glow, place the map under a bright light for about
two minutes. When the map is fully charged, turn off the lights (the darker
the room the better) and see the stars glow. Try to find each of the zodiac
constellations with the lights out. Now turn on the light to see how well you did.
Could you find them all?

Dot TO Dot
IN THE Sky

STORIES OF THE ZODIAC

Joan Marie Galat

illustrations by
Lorna Bennett

whitecap

For additional information, please contact Whitecap Books Ltd.,
351 Lynn Avenue, North Vancouver, British Columbia,
Canada V7J 2C4.

Edited by Kirsten Craven
Proofread by Marilyn Bittman and Ben D'Andrea
Interior design by Roberta Batchelor and Jesse Marchand
Star maps by Five Seventeen
    (after *The Cambridge Star Atlas* by Wil Triton)

Printed and bound in China

Library and Archives Canada Cataloguing in Publication

Galat, Joan Marie, 1963–
Dot to dot in the sky : stories of the zodiac /
Joan Marie Galat ; illustrations by Lorna Bennett.

ISBN 1-55285-805-7
ISBN 978-1-55285-805-9

1. Zodiac—Juvenile literature. I. Bennett, Lorna, 1960–
II. Title.

BF1726.G34 2006   j523   C2006-900700-4

The publisher acknowledges the support of the Canada Council for the Arts, the British
Columbia Arts Council, and the government of Canada through the Book Publishing
Industry Development Program (BPIDP). Whitecap Books also acknowledges the
financial support of the Province of British Columbia through the Book Publishing
Tax Credit.

For my sisters Barbara and Val, with love
— J.M.G.

For Dawn Marie So
— L.B.

Acknowledgments

I am very pleased to recognize the frequent and generous assistance given by Douglas Hube, professor emeritus at the University of Alberta and former national president (1994–96) of the Royal Astronomical Society of Canada.
— J.M.G.

Contents

Astronomy and Astrology of the Zodiac

Since ancient times, people have looked up at the night sky and imagined they could see pictures in groups of stars, called constellations. More than four thousand years ago, the Babylonians divided part of the sky into the 12 constellations of the zodiac to show where the Sun, Moon, and planets appear to travel when seen from Earth. The Greeks spread these symbols to many other cultures.

The area in the sky marked by the zodiac is like a star-studded highway. All the planets except the dwarf planet, Pluto, are always found in or near this orbital pathway, called the ecliptic. From our viewpoint on Earth, the Sun spends close to 30 days in each zodiac constellation and takes a year to complete its apparent path through the sky. We use the term "apparent path" to describe the view we see from our perspective on Earth.

Traditionally the 12 constellations of the zodiac are Aries, Taurus, Gemini, Cancer, Leo, Virgo, Libra, Scorpius, Sagittarius, Capricornus, Aquarius, and Pisces. You may recognize these as the same names used in astrology for horoscopes.

People often confuse astronomy and astrology, which are two different things. Astronomy is a science that focuses on studying the celestial objects found in the sky beyond Earth's atmosphere. Astronomers examine what these objects are made of and where they might come from, as well as their appearance, motion, and distance.

Founded on the zodiac constellations, astrology is the ancient belief that the positions of the stars, planets, Sun, and Moon influence character and destiny. People of ancient cultures looked at the night sky and imagined the constellations as important symbols relating to their many gods. They thought the stars might also symbolize events in their lives.

In astrology, horoscopes are created by examining the positions of celestial objects at the exact moment of your birth, as well as throughout your life. Everyone has a zodiac sign, depending on which constellation the Sun was in at the time of birth.

Scientists do not believe that horoscopes can be used to understand people's behavior and predict the future. Although scientists think the notion of astrology is nonsense, the zodiac constellations are still recognized as important because they help us map the sky and describe the locations of the Sun, Moon, planets, and other night sky objects.

Astrology was developed in different places around the world, including India and Central America. One of the first types of astrology was developed around 3000 BC by people known as the Chaldeans of

Babylonia. The Chaldeans lived in an area of the world now known as the country Iraq. The Chinese are known to have used astrology in 2000 BC. Astrology spread to Greece by 500 BC, with Greeks, Romans, and Egyptians developing a system much like the one used today by Western astrologers.

Although the Christian religion did not approve of astrology, it was widely practiced in Europe during the Middle Ages. This period of time lasted from about the years 500 to 1400. Astrology and astronomy were thought to be related sciences until the 1500s, but once scientists like Nicolaus Copernicus and Galileo Galilei learned more about the universe, astronomers realized that astrology was not a science.

You may be familiar with astrology through the horoscopes found in newspapers. Usually only a few short sentences, these horoscopes tell you about your personality and warn you about events that might happen to you during the day or the coming week. Horoscopes can be a lot of fun to read, but they are often written in such a general way that they will have meaning for many people. If you read the horoscope of every sign, you will probably discover something that applies to you in each one!

Astrology can be an entertaining way to explore your personality, but it is not a science. No one has ever proven that astrology can be used to predict the future or accurately describe each person's personality based on their birth date. Whatever you believe, it is important to recognize that your response to what happens in your life is really a matter of personal choice. It is not something beyond your control that happens because of the locations of objects in the sky.

The zodiac constellations are interesting for another reason. Like most of the star groups that make up the 88 official constellations, the zodiac stars are associated with myths and legends that tell the adventures of ancient gods, animals, and heroes. These stories were created to explain events that ancient cultures did not understand, such as weather and the changing seasons. Ancient stories were also used to explore and describe human emotions.

Search for the zodiac constellations by connecting the stars dot-to-dot in the sky. Imagine the stories that originated long ago, as people gazed up at the same star patterns you see today!

Your Sign

Your sun sign, which is also called your zodiac sign, is determined by the location of the Sun in the zodiac at the time of your birth. For example, if your birthday is on November 18, you are born under the zodiac sign of Scorpius.

The Sun actually moves through 13 constellations, not 12. It is in the constellation Ophiuchus for about 18 days each year. Some of the planets you can see with the naked eye pass through the constellations Cetus, Corvus, Scutum, Auriga, Crater, Orion, Serpens, Pegasus, Sextans, Canis Minor, and Hydra. The dwarf planet Pluto goes through the constellations Boötes, Coma Berenices, Eridanus, and Leo Minor.

ASTRONOMY NAMES AND NUMBERS

- Many of the 88 official constellations are based on Greek and Roman history, although cultures from around the world have also named star groups after animals, objects, and legends from their own regions.

- The individual stars first linked with mythology were usually named using the Greek, Arabic, or Egyptian languages. Stars usually have more than one name because they were seen by ancient cultures in many different places around the world. These names are often still used, but stars are also numbered to avoid confusion. Numbering systems are based on the star's location and luminosity—its total brightness. Today astronomers who belong to the International Astronomical Union officially name stars. You may notice that certain books describe differing ages or distances for the same stars. This is because some books state the number of stars that can be seen with binoculars or a small telescope, while others refer to what can be seen with large professional instruments.

- A comet is a celestial object made up of ice, rock, and dust that orbits the Sun. French astronomer Charles Messier published a catalogue of sky objects more than two hundred years ago. He was looking for comets and made the list so that people using small telescopes would know these objects were not comets. Currently there are 110 Messier objects. You can see a few of the brightest ones with the naked eye. Most Messier objects look like dim white patches of light when seen through a refractor telescope with a 60–70 millimeter diameter. Their names always start with the letter "M" followed by a number. For example, M4 in Scorpius is a globular cluster of hundreds of thousands of stars held together by gravity.

- The equator is an imaginary circle around Earth that divides north and south. The angular distance north or south of the equator, called latitude, is measured in degrees. You can see up to about 180 degrees of the sky if there are no trees or buildings blocking your view of Earth's horizon.

- The zodiac constellations are centered on the ecliptic. The constellations extend eight degrees on either side of the ecliptic.

Changing View of the Stars

Our view of the stars gradually changes over many thousands of years because Earth's axis is moving. Called precession, this movement occurs because gravity from the Sun and Moon make Earth wobble. Earth's axis completes one circle in 25,800 years. Because Earth's axis is slowly shifting, the Sun no longer appears in each zodiac constellation on the dates described in horoscopes.

This means that astrologers who write horoscopes for newspapers base their predictions on star positions that are thousands of years out of date. Your sign is really one constellation "earlier" than described when the zodiac constellations were first defined, which makes your sign one constellation earlier than shown in a newspaper horoscope. For example, even if your birthday falls under Scorpio in the Western Sun Sign chart, you are really a Libra. This is another reason why astrology is unscientific.

Direction of Precession

Earth's Rotation

Earth's Axis

Direction of Precession

Some astrologers consider Ophiuchus, the Serpent Bearer, to be the zodiac's 13th constellation. Due to the effects of Earth's precession, the Sun is in front of the stars of Ophiuchus during the first half of December.

You can predict the location of the closest star to Earth—the Sun. By looking for the constellation behind the Full Moon, you can discover where the Sun is located six months earlier and later. From our view on Earth, the Full Moon is nearly opposite the Sun.

Astrology

- Ancient skygazers knew only about the Sun, Moon, Mercury, Venus, Mars, Jupiter, and Saturn. When Uranus, Neptune, and Pluto were discovered, astrologers had to reconsider how these celestial objects influenced horoscopes.

- Astrology fascinates many people because it is natural to be curious about ourselves, our relationships with other people, and the future. Astrology may have developed when ancient people noticed the stars and other celestial objects occurred in certain patterns at the same time as important events in their lives. This could have led them to believe in a connection between their experiences and the objects in the night sky.

Zodiac Constellation Dates

Constellation Name The constellation and Western sun sign names are the same.	Chinese Moon Sign Chinese Moon signs follow the same dates as Western sun signs.	Western Sun Sign Dates These dates are the same as those described in newspaper horoscopes. They show the original dates of the Sun in the zodiac constellations.	Modern Dates of the Sun in the Zodiac Constellation These dates indicate your real sign.	Number of Days the Sun Is in Each Constellation
Sagittarius	Dragon	Nov 22–Dec 21	Dec 18–Jan 18	32
Capricornus	Snake	Dec 22–Jan 19	Jan 19–Feb 15	28
Aquarius	Horse	Jan 20–Feb 18	Feb 16–Mar 11	24
Pisces	Sheep	Feb 19–Mar 20	Mar 12–Apr 18	38
Aries	Monkey	Mar 21–Apr 19	Apr 19–May 13	25
Taurus	Rooster	Apr 20–May 20	May 14–Jun 19	37
Gemini	Dog	May 21–Jun 21	Jun 20–Jul 20	31
Cancer	Pig	Jun 22–Jul 22	Jul 21–Aug 9	20
Leo	Rat	Jul 23–Aug 22	Aug 10–Sep 15	37
Virgo	Ox	Aug 23–Sep 22	Sep 16–Oct 30	45
Libra	Tiger	Sep 23–Oct 22	Oct 31–Nov 22	23
Scorpius	Rabbit	Oct 23–Nov 21	Nov 23–Nov 29	7
Ophiuchus			Nov 30–Dec 17	18

Stargazing

Before you go outside to stargaze, make a checklist of the stars, planets, and other celestial objects you hope to identify in the night sky. Dress warmly! Clear starry nights are often cool because there are no clouds to trap the sun-warmed air near Earth. If the weather is very cold, plan ahead by setting up a sleeping bag on a reclining lawn chair. Make sure you have everything you need, so you do not spoil your ability to see in the dark by going in and out of lit areas.

Once you are outside, you can improve your night vision by giving your eyes at least 15 minutes to get used to the dark. Use a flashlight with a red lens when you are looking at star charts. The red light helps your night vision by allowing the pupils in your eyes to stay adjusted to the dark. If you do not have a flashlight with a red lens, wrap a red plastic bag over the beam of your flashlight and hold the plastic in place with a rubber band. You will know your eyes have adapted to the dark when you can see each star of the Little Dipper. If you still cannot see all of the Little Dipper's stars after 15 minutes, the place you have chosen to stargaze may not be dark enough to see some of the dimmer night sky objects.

You will easily spot meteors from a dark location. Meteors are often called falling stars or shooting stars, but they are really fragments of rock and dust that burn up as they enter Earth's atmosphere. A pebble-sized meteor can produce a light as bright as a Full Moon. These very bright meteors are called fireballs. You can expect to see

The Milky Way Galaxy

- A galaxy is a gigantic, rotating collection of stars, gas, and dust drawn together by gravity. The Milky Way Galaxy has more than two hundred billion stars and includes all the stars we can see with the naked eye. Because its stars are so far away, it appears as a roadway of sparkling light winding through the night sky.

- You can see the Milky Way from both hemispheres. The closer you are to the equator, the more of the Milky Way you will see. In summer, observers in the northern hemisphere can see the galaxy's center, where there are more stars and gas. In winter, northern hemisphere observers look toward the outer edge of the galaxy.

This area of the Milky Way is not as bright as the part seen during the summer. People in the southern hemisphere can view the constellation Sagittarius, which is in the center of the Milky Way, during their fall, winter, and spring.

- New stars are formed in clouds of dust and gas called nebulae. Stars are born when gravity causes huge clouds of dust and gas to collapse. This creates incomplete stars called protostars, which eventually contract, drawing together to create stars like our Sun.

- An aging star burns up hydrogen, then helium. It becomes larger, cooler, and brighter than our Sun. This aging star is called a red giant or red supergiant, depending on its size. These giant stars eventually collapse and may explode. Depending on its original mass, a red giant or red supergiant might become a white dwarf, a small star that at first is very hot. They could also become neutron stars, which are very small, dense stars with intense gravity. Neutron stars have diameters of about 40–60 kilometers (60–100 miles). Red giants or red supergiants can also collapse to form black holes, objects with such strong gravity that nothing can escape, not even light.

four or five meteors per hour on any dark, clear night.

Many meteors become visible several times each year when a meteor shower occurs. On these nights you might see a few dozen to one hundred or more meteors each hour. If you trace the trails of these meteors backward, they will appear to come from a constellation. This constellation gives the meteor shower its name. For example, a meteor shower called the Capricornids appears to originate in the constellation Capricornus. Try to look around the constellation instead of directly into it. You will see longer light trails and spot more meteors that are dim.

You do not need special equipment to see a constellation. In fact, you cannot find most constellations using a telescope or binoculars because star groups are quite spread out! Using a telescope or binoculars is helpful when you are observing multiple star systems or looking for deep sky objects, such as star clusters, galaxies, and nebulae. Binoculars are easier to use than a telescope and are the best way to explore the sky before investing money in a telescope. When buying binoculars, make sure they are light enough for you to hold steady for long periods of time.

Astronomers describe stars according to their brightness, which is called magnitude. The dimmer the star, the higher its magnitude. Stars that can barely be seen with the naked eye are called "sixth magnitude" stars. Whether or not you can see a star in the sky depends on how dark it is, as well as the skill of the observer.

Generally you can use 10 x 50 binoculars to spot up to ninth magnitude stars on a dark night. A good amateur telescope with a solid footing, such as a 75-millimeter (3-inch) refractor telescope, will allow you to see 12th magnitude stars. A 100-millimeter (4-inch) reflector telescope will show you approximately 12.5 magnitude stars.

Zodiac Personalities

Virgo

Astrologers describe those born between August 23 and September 22 as:
- observant, practical, and hard-working
- well-dressed, tidy, and organized
- good communicators, though sometimes shy and critical
- smart and loving

Libra

Astrologers describe those born between September 23 and October 22 as:
- thoughtful, gracious, and intelligent
- enjoying luxury and making people happy
- meddling, but also skilled peacemakers who like to avoid confrontations
- pleasant, attractive, and outgoing

Scorpius

Astrologers describe those born between October 23 and November 21 as:
- energetic, observant, and thoughtful
- sensitive, intense, and mysterious
- leaders and risk takers
- strong-willed, loyal, and capable of genius

Sagittarius

Astrologers describe those born between November 22 and December 21 as:
- playful, friendly, and cheerful
- honest and truth-seeking
- kind, but sometimes tactless
- optimistic, lucky, and giving

Capricornus

Astrologers describe those born between December 22 and January 19 as:
- dependable, sensible, and careful
- solemn and hard-working
- unapproachable, shy, and sometimes awkward
- ambitious, motivated, and disciplined

Aquarius

Astrologers describe those born between January 20 and February 18 as:
- talented, inventive, and creative
- inquisitive, friendly, and playful
- indifferent and unsympathetic
- independent, shrewd, and flexible

Pisces

Astrologers describe those born between February 19 and March 20 as:
- sensitive, emotional, and dreamy
- imaginative, easygoing, and adaptable
- evasive and gullible
- good listeners, fair, and sympathetic

Aries

Astrologers describe those born between March 21 and April 19 as:
- confident, quick-witted, and brave
- alert, energetic, and outspoken
- obstinate and hasty
- enjoying challenges, adventure, and action

Taurus

Astrologers describe those born between April 20 and May 20 as:
- gentle, artistic, and sentimental
- patient, warm-hearted, and cheerful
- reliable, persistent, and stubborn
- not fond of change or uncertainty

Gemini

Astrologers describe those born between May 21 and June 21 as:
- adaptable, intelligent, and well-read
- sometimes sly, mischievous, and restless
- enjoying storytelling and doing many things at once
- chatty, lively, and witty

Cancer

Astrologers describe those born between June 22 and July 22 as:
- encouraging, home-loving, and caring
- artistic, imaginative, and sensitive
- emotional, moody, and likely to worry
- having an excellent memory

Leo

Astrologers describe those born between July 23 and August 22 as:
- sensitive, generous, kind, and protective of others
- good at organizing and leading
- self-centered, with a strong need to be noticed
- enjoying admiration and having fun

Use the dot-to-dot patterns on the following pages to find the constellations of the zodiac. You do not have to count or see every star in the picture to have found a constellation. Some stars are fainter than others because they are less luminous or farther away. Even a Crescent Moon can cast enough light to make some stars invisible.

When you look at the constellation chart in this book, you will notice that some stars are drawn larger than others. These represent the brighter stars in the sky. It will be easier to find the entire constellation if you look for the brightest stars first.

Each zodiac constellation is best seen at certain times of the year. The best season for early evening viewing is listed after each constellation. You might also be able to see the constellation during other seasons, but at a different time of night. Some constellations, especially those of the zodiac, may not be visible in other seasons because they are below the horizon.

A constellation in the sky may appear at a different angle than shown in the illustrations because of your location and the rotation of Earth. Each season can change its orientation. You may have to try tilting your head to make it easier to spot the shape of a constellation if it is not at the same angle as shown in the picture.

From the equator, you can see all of the constellations, over the course of a year. If you are north or south of the equator, you can see all of the constellations in your hemisphere over the course of a year. Another way to see all of the constellations that are visible from your location is to stay up all night! Just as the Sun rises in the east and sets in the west, the stars at night also rise in the east and set in the west.

GET STARTED

You need to find only one constellation to get started. Once you are able to find the constellations in the diagrams, you can use the Constellation Chart to locate even more.

The Big Dipper is part of the constellation called Ursa Major. It is the starting point for finding several constellations because it is one of the easiest star patterns to find. Face north and look up. Search the northern sky for the seven distinct stars that form the Big Dipper. If you cannot find it this way, remember: one dipper can always help you find the other.

The Little Dipper is called Ursa Minor. It is an important constellation because it is the home of Polaris, the North Star. If you were at the North Pole and looked straight up, Polaris would be the star almost directly overhead. You can find Polaris by following the pointer stars from the Big Dipper.

You can also try to find Polaris this way: face north and hold your fist straight out in front of you. The distance from your index knuckle to your pinky knuckle equals about 10 degrees. Now go hand-over-hand with your fists the same number of degrees as your latitude.

You can find your latitude on a globe or map of Earth by finding your location on the map and looking for the number next to the closest latitude line. For example, if you live 50 degrees north of the equator, you would go hand-over-hand with your fists five times. Once you do this, your top fist will be pointing at the patch of sky where Polaris is found, at the end of the Little Dipper's handle.

The two stars on the other end of the Little Dipper are called the guard stars. Polaris and the guard stars are brighter than the rest of the Little Dipper. Once you see Polaris and the guard stars, connect the dots to find the other stars in this constellation.

Now you are ready to find Virgo and the rest of the zodiac stars by following the directions under each zodiac constellation.

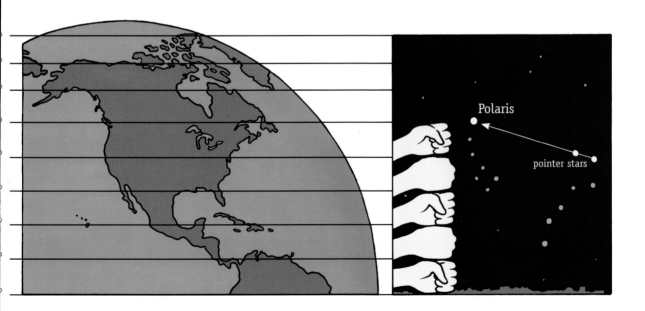

Virgo: The Virgin
Sixth Sign of the Zodiac

Ancient Roman mythology describes five different stages of human existence. These periods are called the "Ages of Man." The first Age of Man was the Golden Age that took place during the reign of Cronus, the ruler of the first gods and the giants called Titans. During this age the Earth provided everything that was needed for humans to live. Nobody had to work, no one ever became sick, and animals lived together in harmony. Farming was not necessary, and arts and crafts were not made. It was always springtime in the Golden Age—a period of eternal peace, innocence, and happiness.

During the Golden Age the god Zeus and goddess Themis had a daughter named Astraea, which means "star maiden." Like Themis, Astraea became a goddess of justice. She used the scales of Libra to weigh the good and bad of men. During the Golden Age there were no human women. Astraea enjoyed living on the Earth during the Golden Age because it was a time of truth and justice. There were no wars and no fighting over possessions. Everyone happily shared everything.

Gradually a new race of people appeared on the Earth and the Golden Age became the Silver Age. These years were mostly pleasant, but not as magnificent as the Golden Age. Zeus overthrew Cronus and became the new ruler of all the gods. He shortened spring and created different seasons. Cooler weather meant men had to build houses to protect themselves. For the first time, nature no longer provided everything. During the Silver Age, women

SPACE NOTES

First magnitude Spica is 260 light-years away from Earth and 2,100 times more luminous than the Sun. Spica is a double star system with two close stars orbiting each other every four days. Scientists think Spica may be a multiple star system containing three additional faint stars.

Virgo contains a cluster of about 3,000 galaxies called the Virgo supercluster. It is the nearest supercluster of galaxies to Earth at about 50 million light-years away. There is a region beyond the Virgo supercluster that does not contain many galaxies. This region is called a cosmic void.

○ The sizes of newly discovered planets are often compared to Jupiter, the largest planet in our solar system. Jupiter is 11 times larger in diameter than Earth. If Jupiter was hollow, it could hold 1,323 Earths. There is a planet outside our solar system that is at least 6.6 times more massive than Jupiter. It orbits 70 Virginis, a visible fifth magnitude star in Virgo. The planet completes one orbit around 70 Virginis every 117 days.

○ The equinox occurs twice each year, everywhere on Earth, when the Sun crosses the equator and makes day and night of nearly equal length. The autumn equinox occurs in Virgo around September 21 when the Sun crosses the ecliptic from north to south.

- Remember the useful saying, "Arc to Arcturus and speed on to Spica," to jump from the Big Dipper in Ursa Major, to Arcturus in Boötes, the Herdsman, and on to Spica, the brightest star in Virgo.

- Look for the goddess of justice, Virgo, between Leo and Libra. You can reach Virgo from Leo by leaping from Regulus to blue Spica. Another way to find Virgo is to start in Libra and make a line from either Zubeneschamali or Zubenelgenubi to Spica.

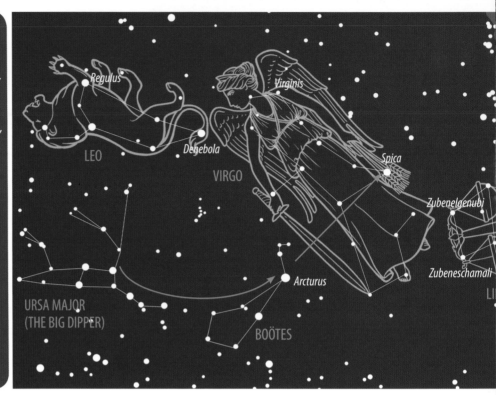

came to the Earth for the first time. People began to fight and live shorter lives. They did not worship the gods as often as before and sometimes ignored them completely. Astraea was unhappy with the changes and no longer wanted to live among mortals—people who were unable to live forever. She moved to the home of the gods and goddesses on Mount Olympus, but still visited the Earth to weigh the good and bad deeds of the people, as well as demand justice for their crimes.

The Silver Age eventually ended, which led to the Brazen Age. In this age men made weapons and fought with each other

even more, sometimes starting bloody wars. The Iron Age followed the Brazen Age and was the most difficult time to be on the Earth. Crime became commonplace as modesty, truth, and honor vanished.

The gods and goddesses got tired of humans, with all their violence and dishonesty. Astraea was the last goddess to continue visiting the Earth, but eventually even she found the behavior of humans too terrible to endure. The goddess of justice fled to the heavens. You can still see Astraea in the stars of Virgo. She is near Libra, which represents the scales Astraea used to weigh justice.

Libra: The Scales
Seventh Sign of the Zodiac

The ancient Greeks did not develop a myth specifically about the scales represented by Libra, but during the Roman Empire the scales were said to weigh day and night during the autumn equinox. The equal length of day and night at this time of the year balanced the scales.

Virgo, the goddess of justice, was thought to weigh people's souls. The scales told her whether to send them to a place for punishment or eternal happiness.

Libra is the only zodiac sign that does not represent something living. It was the last zodiac sign to be named.

The stars of Libra originally marked the Scorpion's claws. Libra's two brightest stars, Zubenelgenubi and Zubeneschamali, have Arabic names. Zubenelgenubi means "southern claw." Zubeneschamali means "northern claw." Zubenelgenubi is about 77 light-years away from Earth, and Zubeneschamali is about 160 light-years away.

A planet orbits a star called 23 Librae, which is found in the southeast corner of Libra. The planet is about 1.6 times the mass of Jupiter. It takes 260 days to orbit 23 Librae—a faint sixth magnitude star that is 84 light-years away from Earth. This star is close to the size of our Sun, but older. The Sun is five billion years old, while 23 Librae is nearly nine billion years old.

OBSERVING ZODIACAL LIGHT

Virgo who used the scales of Libra

- Zodiacal light is a faint glow that occurs near Earth's horizon when sunlight reflects off dust particles orbiting the Sun. Chunks of rock or metal in space, called asteroids, form dust particles when they collide with each other. Dust particles also occur when matter separates from a comet's melting ice as it passes near the Sun.

- You can see zodiacal light before sunrise and after sunset. Zodiacal light has a triangular shape, unlike sunshine and light pollution. The glow of zodiacal light is easiest to see from very dark locations in the evening sky during spring. It is easier for people living at lower latitudes to see zodiacal light. If you live in the northern hemisphere, look for zodiacal light on March evenings and September mornings. If you live in the southern hemisphere, look for it on September evenings and March mornings.

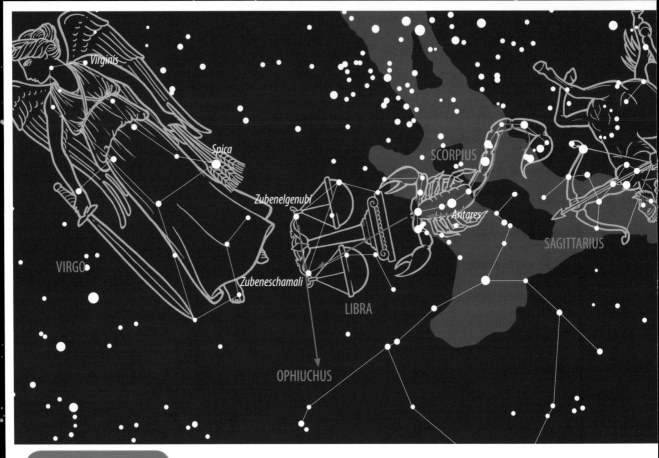

Virginis

Spica

Zubenelgenubi

SCORPIUS

Antares

VIRGO

Zubeneschamali

SAGITTARIUS

LIBRA

OPHIUCHUS

Find Libra

Northern hemisphere: spring

Southern hemisphere: autumn

- Libra is between Virgo and Scorpius. Look for Libra by starting at the brighter stars of Scorpius and leaping to the stars that form the scales. You can also find Libra by following a line from Spica, in Virgo, to Libra's brighter stars, Zubeneschamali or Zubenelgenubi.

- Try to search for the constellation Ophiuchus, which is sometimes called the 13th zodiac sign, by making a line through Zubeneschamali and Zubenelgenubi to the large shape of the physician.

Scorpius: The Scorpion
Eighth Sign of the Zodiac

According to Greek mythology, Poseidon, god of the sea, and a Gorgon called Euryale had a handsome son named Orion. He grew into a giant and became a mighty hunter. Orion liked to scout for animals with Artemis, the goddess of wild animals and the Moon. One day Orion bragged he was so great he could hunt and kill every animal on the Earth.

Artemis was shocked to hear Orion's brazen claim. Mother Earth, who was called Gaia, learned of Orion's bragging and also became very upset. She imagined the Earth without a single animal upon it and pictured a world without joy or pleasure.

Gaia vowed to stop Orion. She was determined to protect each and every animal but knew the task would require great cunning. After much thought Gaia decided she needed a helper who would be small enough to get close to Orion without being seen. She chose the Scorpion because it loves to scurry about in dark places.

The Scorpion looked for Orion and found him in a field on the edge of a forest. Orion was hunting alone because Artemis no longer enjoyed his company. Slowly and carefully the Scorpion worked its way closer to Orion until at last it was near the giant's feet. Carefully aiming the tip of his tail, the Scorpion stung Orion's heel. The poison moved quickly through the giant's body.

As Orion fell to the ground the great physician Aesculapius emerged from the forest where he had been gathering plants to make medicine. Aesculapius gave Orion a magical herb he had discovered in the mouth of a snake. His remedy immediately stopped the poison from working and Orion's life was saved. He did not realize he was interfering with the will of the gods.

Gaia was not the only one to become angry when she found out Aesculapius had helped Orion. Hades, the king of the underworld and ruler of dead souls, knew his empire would shrink if Aesculapius went around restoring life. He complained to Zeus, the king of the gods, who agreed that Aesculapius should not interfere in matters of life and death. Zeus called for Aquila, the

---

You can see the story of the battle between life and death told in the stars.

- When Scorpius sets in the sky, Ophiuchus looks as if he is about to crush the creature with his foot. This symbolizes that the doctor's strength is greater than the animal's poison.

- After Ophiuchus cures the giant, Orion rises in the east.

- When the stars of the constellation Aquila are overhead, imagine the Eagle hurling the thunderbolt. Ophiuchus sinks below the horizon, making it appear that the doctor has died.

- The stars of Scorpius rise in the east as if the Scorpion is planning to approach Orion again, but the Scorpion and Hunter remain on opposite sides of the sky.

- Scorpius sets in the west, as Orion rises in the east, restored to life by Ophiuchus.

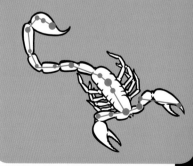

Find Scorpius

Northern hemisphere: spring

Southern hemisphere: autumn

- Scorpius is between Libra and Sagittarius, and directly below Ophiuchus. Its stars look like a scorpion, complete with a tail and stinger. Scorpius has been described as the most splendid zodiac constellation. It contains many bright stars and resembles its name more than any other zodiac star group. Because Scorpius is found low in the southern horizon, only parts of it are visible from middle and high northern latitudes.

- You can find Scorpius by following a line from the star Zubeneschamali in Libra to the bright red star Antares in Scorpius. Connect the dots in the sky from Sagittarius's brighter stars by making a line to bright red Antares.

Eagle, and ordered him to take one of his thunderbolts and find Aesculapius. Aquila found him in the forest and hurled the thunderbolt, striking Aesculapius dead.

Zeus honored the doctor for his knowledge by placing him in the sky as Ophiuchus, the snake bearer. Scorpius and Orion are on opposite sides of the sky so they will not fight again.

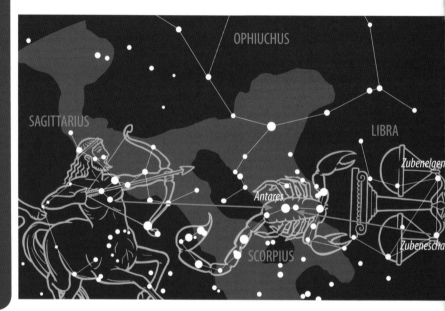

SPACE NOTES

- Red Antares is the 13th brightest star in the sky. Marking the heart of the Scorpion, this first magnitude star is a massive supergiant about 300 times the size of our Sun. One day it will explode into a supernova and become very bright. This explosion could happen anytime, from now to one million years from now.

- The name Antares means "rival of Mars." People sometimes confuse the red star Antares with the red planet Mars because of its color and location in the zodiac.

- A planet estimated to be at least as massive as Jupiter orbits a star in Scorpius called HR 6094. HR 6094 is a dwarf—a small star of average or below-average

brightness. It takes the planet almost 1.5 years to complete one orbit around HR 6094.

- Doctors and other people who work in health-related jobs use a picture of a snake twisted around a staff to symbolize their work in medicine. The symbol comes from Aesculapius, the Greek healer who saved Orion from the Scorpion's venom.

Sagittarius: The Archer
Ninth Sign of the Zodiac

Although Sagittarius means archer, the constellation is a centaur with the chest, arms, and head of a man, but the body and legs of a horse. Centaurs were followers of Dionysus, the god of wine. Most were rowdy, wild creatures that liked to fight. They were prone to drunkenness and could not be trusted in any way.

Chiron was different than the others of his clan. He was the wisest of all centaurs, famous for being just, as well as excelling in shooting, healing, music, and prophecy. Chiron shared his knowledge with others and instructed many students. One was Aesculapius, who became the great physician. Another was the hero Hercules.

In the midst of a quest to become immortal, Hercules was beginning his fourth task, to capture the wild boar terrorizing the mountains of Erymanthus. His travels brought him through northern Greece to Mount Pelion in Thessaly, the land where centaurs lived.

Hercules stopped to rest at the home of a centaur named Philon. The hero was thirsty and Philon kindly offered him a drink. Unfortunately, the wine he served was not his alone to share. It belonged to all the centaurs and when Philon opened the cask, the rich fragrance of wine filled the air with such a strong scent that the other centaurs smelled it and galloped to Philon's house. The centaurs were furious to discover he had shared the wine without their permission and shouted insults at Philon and Hercules.

The yelling turned to angry shoving. Hercules raised his club to force the centaurs back, but that only made them wilder. They continued crowding up to him, shouting taunts and daring him to fight until he pulled out his bow and arrows. The arrows had been dipped in the Hydra's poisonous blood and were so toxic that anyone whose skin was pierced would instantly be overcome with agonizing pain. The centaurs backed away, turning to flee when Hercules drew his first arrow against the bow.

Hercules gave chase and the centaurs scattered, one group running towards Chiron's house for safety. The famed centaur was outside, trying to see what

SPACE NOTES

- The Little Milk Dipper's handle is in the Milky Way, as if someone is scooping up milk to serve with the tea in the Teapot.

- In ancient Greek mythology a centaur is a half-man, half-horse creature. In astronomy a centaur is a type of celestial object that has the same characteristics as both comets and asteroids.

- Sagittarius contains 15 Messier objects, including globular clusters, open clusters, and gaseous nebulae. The Lagoon Nebula, M8, is large and bright enough to be seen with the naked eye.

Find Sagittarius

Northern hemisphere: summer

Southern hemisphere: winter

- Sagittarius is between Scorpio and Capricornus. Find Sagittarius by looking just northeast of the Scorpion's stinger. The brightest stars in Sagittarius form the shape of a teapot. It looks as though tea is being poured into the Scorpion's tail. The stars that make up the Teapot are called an asterism—a collection of stars that form a picture within a constellation.

- The stars of the Teapot make the Little Milk Dipper, the Bow, and the Arrow. The Arrow points to the center of the Milky Way.

- Lying in the brightest part of the Milky Way, Sagittarius is the most southern zodiac constellation in the southern hemisphere.

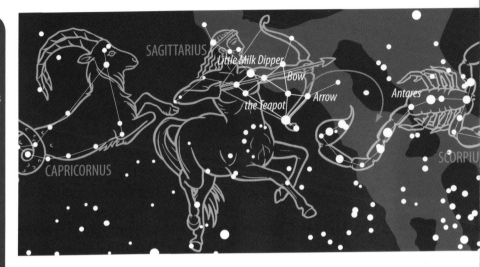

all the noise was about, when the others came upon him. Still firing arrows, Hercules did not recognize his friend among the other centaurs and continued firing arrows as the centaurs took off in different directions. His arrow struck one centaur, who fell to the ground. It was Chiron. Waves of pain coursed through his body, the agony instantly unbearable.

Hercules felt sick when he saw what he had done. He knew Chiron could not escape this torture through death. As an immortal being, the centaur would be cursed to suffer for all time.

Frantic for relief, Chiron prayed to Zeus, asking to

exchange his immortality for death. Zeus felt sorry for the wise centaur and allowed him to give his immortality to the Titan, Prometheus.

Zeus honored Chiron by placing him in the stars as Sagittarius, the Archer. Sagittarius points his bow and arrow at Antares, the bright star in the heart of Scorpio. One myth claims he shoots the Scorpion to avenge Orion, who suffered its sting.

Chiron represents ancient wisdom and symbolizes the strength of the wild horse, tamed to serve man. The constellation called Centaur is also associated with Chiron.

Capricornus: The Sea Goat
10th Sign of the Zodiac

Typhon was the most ferocious giant born after Zeus overthrew the early gods of the Golden Age. He was the son of Mother Earth, called Gaia, and the Titan, Tartarus. Typhon was tall enough to reach the stars and strong enough to throw a mountain after ripping it from the ground. He had hundreds of fire-breathing dragon heads that spewed molten lava and flaming rocks from each mouth. Poison dripped from the eyes of each dragon head. Typhon's body was covered in twisting hissing snakes whose tongues darted in and out.

Typhon's mate was called Echidna. She was half-woman, half-serpent. Both Typhon and Echidna were so fearful that even the gods ran way at the sight of them. One day Typhon was in a fierce mood and decided to attack the gods of Mount Olympus. He bellowed in anger as he looked for them, his voice louder than all other sounds. The gods were enjoying a picnic beside the Nile River when they heard the monster bellowing. Realizing Typhon was coming their way, the terrified gods used their powers to turn themselves into different creatures as they fled the mountain. The king of the gods, Zeus, took the form of a ram. Hermes became a bird called an ibis and Apollo flew away as a black crow. The goddess Hera transformed herself into a cow and the god Dionysus turned himself into a goat, while the goddess Aphrodite and the god Eros became fish.

Typhon turned toward the Nile River, where Pan stood in the form of a goat. A merry god, Pan was always in love with different nymphs, but the beautiful maidens always rejected him because he was so ugly. Pan saw Typhon coming and jumped into the river in panic. He tried to turn himself into a fish but failed because he was so flustered. Instead, Pan's bottom half became a fish tail and his top half remained a billy goat, complete with two horns and a beard.

Pan raised his head above the water to see if he was safe and saw Zeus had returned in his own form to fight Typhon. The

SPACE NOTES

- About 2,000 years ago, the Sun passed in front of Capricornus when it reached its winter solstice, or lowest point in the sky. The latitude called the Tropic of Capricornus was the most southerly place the Sun appeared directly overhead. Due to Earth's precession, the winter solstice now occurs when the Sun passes in front of Sagittarius.

- A meteor shower called the Capricornids occurs every year from July 18 to July 30. Under a dark sky you can expect to see up to 15 meteors per hour appearing to stream from Capricornus. Frequently bright and often yellow, the Capricornids sometimes produce spectacular fireballs.

AQUARIUS

Little Milk Dipper

SAGITTARIUS

CAPRICORNUS

monster had removed Zeus's arm and leg muscles and was flinging them about. Without muscles, Zeus was paralyzed and forced to lie powerless on the ground.

Pan pulled himself out of the water and reached for his reed pipe. Usually the music he played on the pipe was so beautiful that it was compared to the song of the nightingale. This time he took a deep breath and blew into the reed pipe with such force that a vile piercing sound filled all of Olympus. Typhon could not bear the sound and was forced to retreat.

Hermes, the messenger god, heard Pan's whistle and flew up on his winged sandals to see what was happening. He saw Zeus lying motionless on the ground and called Pan to come and help. They carefully gathered up Zeus's muscles, positioned them in his body, and tied them back into place.

As soon as Zeus could move, he jumped up, gathered his mightiest thunderbolts, and left to seek revenge. Typhon had already traveled a great distance, but sharp-eyed Zeus soon spotted the giant. He chose his deadliest thunderbolt, took careful aim, and hurled it at Typhon. The thunderbolt crackled through the air, striking Typhon with such intensity that he was driven down into the Earth. Typhon lay where he landed for a very long time, licking his wounds until he could finally lift his head.

Zeus showed his appreciation to Pan by placing him in the stars as the constellation Capricornus. Pan was the god of flocks, shepherds, forests, wildlife, and fertility.

Aquarius: The Water Carrier
11th Sign of the Zodiac

Prometheus, the god of fire, made the first man and woman on Earth from clay. Zeus, king of the gods, brought them to life. Prometheus loved his creation very much and taught people many things. He showed them how to farm the land, make medicine from plants, and tame horses.

Prometheus wanted to make people's lives easier, while Zeus worried they might become too smart and try to take over his throne. When Prometheus suggested giving people fire, Zeus refused. Prometheus argued people could be trusted, but the king of gods would not change his mind.

Prometheus refused to give up. He stole a glowing piece of coal from the fire on Mount Olympus and shared it with the people on Earth. Zeus saw smoke rising from the ground and punished Prometheus for disobeying him.

Although Zeus was the protector and ruler of all humans, after some time he became enraged at the people on Earth. He felt they did not show enough respect for the gods and decided to do something about it.

The Titaness, Themis, had the gift of prophecy and saw Zeus's plan. She visited Prometheus in a dream, warning him disaster was going to fall upon Earth and only two would be saved from a deathly punishment. Themis told him to instruct his son, Deucalion, and his wife, Pyrrha, to build a very large boat and fill it with food, water, and supplies.

When Prometheus woke up, he ran to Deucalion and Pyrrha's house and told them about his dream. Bewildered, they were full of questions but Prometheus had no answers. They followed his wishes and built a gigantic boat, loading it with food, fresh water, and all the supplies that might be needed on a long voyage.

The last of the stores had just been loaded when Zeus disguised himself as Aquarius, the water bearer. To punish the people for their ungracious treatment of the gods, Aquarius overturned an urn of water and poured it onto the Earth. The water fell in torrents from the sky until the Earth was flooded. The world became one monstrous sea, and all drowned except the husband and wife in the boat.

Deucalion and Pyrrha floated upon the water, watching in silence as the land disappeared beneath the waves. They had no idea how long the rain would last or whether they would have enough food and fresh water. Nine days and nine nights later the rain stopped and the water began to go down.

As the water got lower, more land appeared and the boat became stuck on Mount Parnassus. Deucalion and Pyrrha stepped off the boat. They were relieved

SPACE NOTES

- Four stars in Aquarius form the letter Y, an asterism representing Aquarius's urn. Imagine water flowing from the urn into the mouth of Piscis Austrinus, the Southern Fish.

- Aquarius inhabits a part of the sky sometimes called "the sea" because it contains so many other water signs, including Eridanus, the Great River; Cetus, the Whale; Pisces, the Fish; Capricornus, the Sea Goat; and Piscis Austrinus, the Southern Fish.

- When the Nile River overflowed, the ancients said Aquarius had dipped his jar into the Nile River. This marked the beginning of spring, which used to begin in ancient Egypt when the Sun passed in front of Aquarius.

- The brightest two stars in Aquarius are yellow supergiants. Sadalmelik, meaning "the lucky stars of the kingdom," is 750 light-years away. Sadalsuud, Arabic for "the luckiest of all of them," is slightly brighter because it is closer at 600 light-years away.

- Aquarius contains the Helix Nebula, which is the closest planetary nebula to Earth at 450 light-years away. It can be seen as a circular patch of light through binoculars.

- A planet at least 1.28 times as large as Jupiter has been discovered orbiting a star in Aquarius. The star is an unnamed 7th magnitude dwarf, 69 light-years away.

- The sixth magnitude star HR 8734 Piscium, seen between Pisces and Aquarius, is 64 light-years away. A planet orbits this sixth magnitude star every 7.11 days.

Northern hemisphere: summer

Southern hemisphere: winter

- Aquarius is between Pisces and Capricornus.

- You can locate Aquarius by looking directly north of Capricornus. You can also make a line jumping to Aquarius from the Circlet—the five stars forming the southern fish of Pisces.

PISCES

Circlet

AQUARIUS

to be on land but frightened to be the only two people on Earth.

They did not know what to do and prayed to Themis for guidance. She answered by replying, "Toss the bones of your mother over your shoulder."

They looked at each other in confusion and Deucalion rubbed his eyes as if that would make things clearer.

"How would I ever find the bones of my mother?" said Pyrrha.

"It must be a riddle," decided Deucalion. "Perhaps it means the bones of Mother Earth."

"It could be Mother Earth!" agreed Pyrrha, "but where are we to find her bones?"

They tried throwing sticks over their shoulders, but when they looked back nothing was different.

They picked up clods of dirt and threw them back, but once again nothing happened.

They gathered handfuls of stones and tossed them over their shoulders. This time, they looked back and saw people. Men had sprung from the stones thrown by Deucalion. Women had sprung from the stones thrown by Pyrrha.

Deucalion and Pyrrha were relieved to share the Earth with others again. The world began anew and this time people were very careful to show their appreciation and respect for the gods who could both give and take life. Their reminder is in the sky in the shape of Aquarius, holding his urn.

There is more than one version of the myth that tells what happened when the giant monster Typhon decided to terrorize the gods of Mount Olympus. In this story, Aphrodite, the goddess of love, and her son Eros were standing near the sea when they saw Typhon. Flames darted out of his hundreds of fire-breathing dragon heads and poison dripped from his many eyes as he approached the mother and son.

Having come to life from sea foam, Aphrodite tried to escape Typhon by jumping into the water and turning into a fish. Eros followed her into the sea and also became a fish. They were worried they might lose each other in the deep water, so they tied their tails together with a long piece of twine. Typhon stood helpless on the shore as Aphrodite and Eros swam away. Although he could endure fire, he could not survive in the sea.

The Pisces constellation represents the escape of Aphrodite and Eros from Typhon. Aphrodite and Eros are also known by their Roman names, Venus and Cupid.

ind Pisces

- orthern hemisphere: autumn
- outhern hemisphere: spring
- Pisces is between Aries and Aquarius. It looks like a very large letter V.
- Find Pisces by imagining a line going north from the easternmost stars of Aquarius to the Circlet—the five stars forming the southern fish of Pisces. You can also start from the triangle shape of Aries and make an imaginary line from the star Hamal, in Aries, to Al Rescha, the star representing the knot in Pisces.

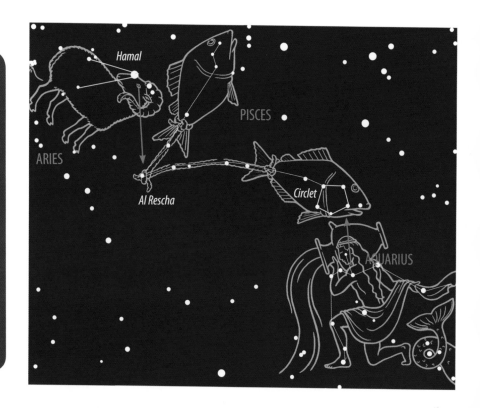

SPACE NOTES

○ The Pisces constellation is spread out in the sky. The two fish look like two roughly shaped diamonds connected with twine. Pisces contains the star Al Rescha, which is Arabic for "the cord." It is seen as a double star system when viewed through a 70-millimeter (3-inch) diameter telescope.

○ In the northern hemisphere the first day of spring occurs during the vernal equinox, around March 21 when the Sun is in Pisces. If we could turn off the Sun for a moment during the month of March, we would see the stars of Pisces lying behind the Sun.

○ A planet at least 6.6 times more massive than Jupiter has been discovered in Pisces. This is the largest known planet. It is so huge that scientists wonder if it might actually be a cool dim star called a brown dwarf. The planet orbits 109 Piscium, a sixth magnitude star that is about eight billion years old and 106 light-years away.

○ Two planets orbit the sixth magnitude star HR 8734 Piscium in the southwest corner of Pisces near its boundary with Aquarius. One of these planets is at least 1.37 times the mass of Jupiter and has a 7.3-day orbit around HR 8734 Piscium. The other planet is at least 2.1 times the mass of Jupiter, with an orbit around the star that takes 3,150 days (8.6 Earth years) to complete. HR 8734 Piscium is 64 light-years away from Earth.

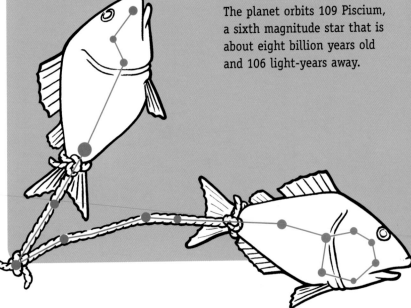

Aries: The Ram
First Sign of the Zodiac

The most beautiful woman on the Earth was Helen. She was the daughter of Zeus and Leda—the Queen of Sparta, who was married to Tyndareus. Helen was so very lovely that every man who saw her wanted her to become his wife. Her suitors were men of noble birth and powerful families. Tyndareus was afraid there would be terrible fighting among the men who wanted to marry Helen. He demanded that each suitor promise loyalty to whomever Helen decided to wed. She chose to marry her richest suitor, who was Menelaus, king of Sparta, and the other suitors accepted their fate.

Paris was the youngest son of Priam and Hecuba, the king and queen of the city of Troy. He fell in love with Helen and spirited her away to the city of Troy, even though she was already married to Menelaus. The Greeks honored their vow to be loyal to Menelaus and prepared to fight for Helen's return. Odysseus, the ruler of the island kingdom of Ithaca, was one of Helen's former suitors. He regretted his oath to Menelaus and did not want to help the other suitors attack Troy. When soldiers came to collect him for battle, Odysseus tried to fool

Find Aries

Northern hemisphere: autumn

Southern hemisphere: spring

- The second smallest zodiac constellation, Aries is between Taurus and Pisces.

- You can look for its hockey stick shape by making an imaginary line up from Al Rescha, the star representing the knot in Pisces. Two bright stars form the handle of the hockey stick and a fainter star forms the blade. You can also reach the Ram by starting at the constellation Taurus and jumping through the star cluster called the Pleiades, or the Seven Sisters.

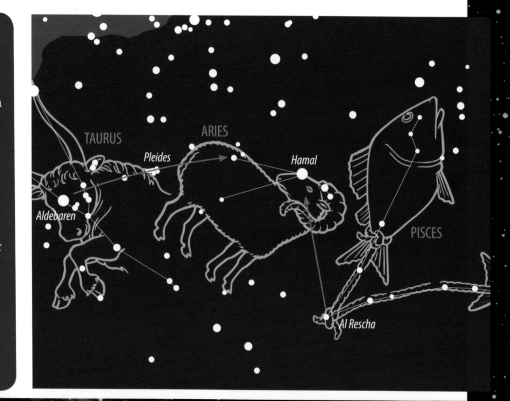

them into thinking he was insane by taking a bag of salt into a field and ploughing the grains into the soil. Odysseus pretended he truly expected the salt to grow. "Is not a grain of salt still a grain?" he asked the onlookers. Uncertain what to do, the soldiers watched until one suspicious man shouted, "Fetch Odysseus's son and set him down in the path of the plough!" Swerving to save his son, Odysseus proved his sanity and was forced to take part in the war to retrieve Helen from the city of Troy.

Odysseus traveled to the Bay of Aulis, where one thousand ships set sail to cross the sea to Troy. As soon as the fleet of ships arrived, the Greek soldiers went ashore and demanded that the Trojans return Helen to Menelaus. The Trojans refused to hand her over. Battle followed battle and death followed death, but neither side would surrender. The war between the Greeks and the Trojans lasted for 10 years.

Although Odysseus had never wanted to join the war, he became one of its leaders and thought of a plan that might end the fighting. He suggested to his troops that they build a wooden horse large enough to hide hundreds of Greek soldiers inside its planks. The Greek soldiers built the wooden horse and dragged it to the beach outside the walls of Troy. Just before sunrise, all of the Greek soldiers who could fit into the horse climbed inside to wait. The rest of the soldiers boarded their ships and sailed out of the harbor.

The Trojans saw the ships leaving and word quickly spread throughout the city. Certain they had finally won, the Trojan soldiers ran down to the beach to make sure that every last Greek was gone. Waving their weapons and cheering, they discovered the beach was bare except for the large wooden horse. Puzzled, they walked around it but, unable to imagine its purpose, decided it must be a peace offering from the Greeks. The Trojan soldiers dragged the horse inside the city gates as a war trophy.

That night everyone in Troy stayed up late, dancing and feasting in celebration. When at last all was quiet, the Greek soldiers climbed out of the horse. They destroyed the city in their surprise attack and ended the war for good. The Greek ships returned to Troy to pick up the soldiers who had stayed behind and Helen was returned to Sparta and Menelaus.

Finally, Odysseus was able to set sail for home, but his journey took 10 years because of the choices he made and the bad luck he encountered along the way. A storm blew his ship off course for so long that Odysseus and his crew became dangerously low on food. Sailing near a mountainous island, Odysseus spotted a cave that looked like someone's shelter.

Hoping to find supplies, he ordered his crew to turn the ship toward shore.

Once on land the soldiers followed a mountain trail to the cave and saw an open gate around the cave's entrance. Odysseus carried a goatskin full of wine that he planned to offer as a gift in return for a friendly welcome and some food.

Passing through the gate, Odysseus and his men saw pens containing lambs and sheep. Further inside the cave they were overjoyed to find buckets of milk and piles of cheese. Feeling certain whoever lived in the cave had more than enough to share, they helped themselves to the food.

Finally, the master of the cave arrived home, trudging heavily as he herded a flock of sheep inside. It was Polyphemus, a Cyclops with a single round eye in his forehead. Cyclops were not known to be friendly creatures. They were stubborn, bad-tempered, fierce giants that behaved without concern for others.

To keep the sheep from roaming outside, Polyphemus rolled a great stone in front of the cave's entrance. After several minutes his eye got used to the dark and he saw the startled faces of Odysseus and his men. He realized they had been gorging on his food and shouted, "Who dares barge into the home of Polyphemus?"

All but Odysseus were too terrified to speak. "We're warriors returning from Troy, under the protection of Zeus," he answered.

The Cyclops became even angrier. "I'm not concerned about Zeus!" he bellowed. Then he reached down, grabbed a man in each of his monstrous hands and chewed them up until there was nothing left. Licking his lips, Polyphemus stretched out on the floor of the cave and fell asleep.

Utterly helpless, the men could only watch and wait. They dared not attack or kill the giant, for even as a group they did not have the strength to move the boulder from the cave's entrance. Odysseus knew the only way to escape would be to outsmart Polyphemus.

Odysseus stayed awake all night, frantically trying to think of a way to save himself and his men. He still did not have an escape plan the next morning and watched in despair as Polyphemus devoured two more men for breakfast. With a satisfied belch, Polyphemus herded his flock into the sunshine and covered the cave's entrance with the stone.

For a brief moment when the stone was rolled away from the entrance, sunshine poured into the cave. It was just enough time for Odysseus to spot a long timber of wood on the floor by the sheep pens. He told his men to cut a goodly length of wood from the timber and sharpen one of its ends. They placed the pointed end of the timber in a fire burning in the cave, turning it again and again in the smoldering coals to make its point hard. When it was ready they let it cool and hid the shaft underneath the smelly sheep dung at the back of the cave.

When Polyphemus returned to the cave that evening, he herded the sheep inside, sealed the entrance with the stone, and without a word of warning, ate two more men.

Odysseus bravely stepped forward and held out a cup filled with wine from his goatskin.

"Polyphemus, would you like to taste the wine I brought from the ship's hold?"

The giant took the cup, tossed the dark liquid down his throat, and demanded more.

Three times Odysseus filled the cup, and three times Polyphemus drank the strong wine down in a single gulp.

"What's your name?" asked Polyphemus.

"I'm called Nobody," replied Odysseus.

"Well, Nobody," replied the Cyclops, "I shall eat you last because you shared your wine." And with that he lay down and fell into a deep drunken sleep.

Odysseus and his men waited until they were sure the giant would not waken. When his snoring became a steady drone, they dug the stake out of its hiding place and heated its point once again. This time the stake got so hot it nearly burst into flames. They carried the stake to where Polyphemus slept and with a great heave that took all their strength, they drove the sizzling stake into the Cyclops's eye. Howling in pain, Polyphemus leapt up in a formidable rage. Screaming and stumbling, he made so much noise that neighboring Cyclops came to see what had happened. Approaching the cave, they shouted to Polyphemus.

"What happened?" one hollered. "Are you under siege?"

"Nobody has attacked me!" shouted Polyphemus. "It's Nobody!"

"If nobody is bothering you, let us sleep," snarled a neighbor, turning toward home with the other Cyclops.

Polyphemus was furious. He tried to find the prisoners in his cave, but they dodged his flailing arms. Feeling his way to the cave's entrance, Polyphemus rolled the stone away from the opening and sat down, knowing the men would try to pass him to escape.

Odysseus already had a plan. Whispering so that Polyphemus would not hear him, he instructed his men to choose thick-fleeced rams and use strips of bark to tie themselves beneath the sheep's bellies. When the sun rose the sheep knew it was time to go to the pasture. They crowded toward the cave's entrance, walked past the Cyclops, and ran out into the sunshine. As each sheep passed, Polyphemus ran his hand over the animal's back to make sure none of the men were riding out. He did not think to feel their bellies, and the men made it safely back to the ship.

Once safely on the water, Odysseus taunted Polyphemus, who was still sitting at the cave's entrance. He shouted across the water, "Well, Cyclops, you're not as smart or strong as you thought! You've lost your sight for eating men who came as your guests!"

Furious, Polyphemus leapt to his feet, tore the peak from his mountain, and hurled the great rock toward Odysseus's voice. The rock almost crushed Odysseus's boat, before the rock sank to the ocean floor, creating a rip tide that sent the ship reeling shoreward. The men used all their strength and skill to fight the current and finally steered the ship back on course, away from the land of the Cyclops.

When their safety at sea was certain, Odysseus called out once more, "You have no eye thanks to me, Odysseus!" Unable to hear him, Polyphemus never found out his opponent was not named "Nobody."

Because the sheep saved Odysseus and his soldiers by bringing them from the dark cave into the light, the constellation Aries, the Ram, came to symbolize the long nights of winter turning into the longer days of spring.

Taurus: The Bull
Second Sign of the Zodiac

Bulls represent strength and fertility in many ancient stories. One Greek myth involving cattle tells the story of Zeus and the beautiful Princess Io, daughter of the river god Inachus. Zeus fell in love with the princess and let her know about his feelings by sending messages of love through her dreams.

Zeus wanted to visit Io but knew his wife Hera would become jealous. To avoid getting caught, Zeus cloaked the Earth in a cloud so black that it seemed as though day had turned to night. Hera saw the cloud and immediately suspected that her deceiving husband was doing something wrong. She searched all of Olympus but could not find him anywhere. Frustrated, the queen of the gods descended to the Earth and commanded the sky to clear. The dark cloud dissolved into wisps of nothingness.

Zeus saw the cloud evaporate and he knew Hera must be nearby. He turned Io into a beautiful white heifer, only seconds before his wife came into sight. Hera walked up to Zeus and stared intently at the young cow.

"Where did this heifer come from?" she finally asked.

"It sprang from the Earth like a newborn, just now!" Zeus lied. "I promise you, I've never seen the creature before this moment."

Hera was not fooled and cleverly asked her husband, "Might I keep this heifer?"

Zeus hesitated. He was desperate to keep Io away from Hera, but could not think of a way to do it. He knew if he refused, Hera would suspect he was doing something wrong. Hera watched him carefully. She asked again, "Will you not give this heifer to me as a gift?" Afraid of her abominable temper, Zeus permitted Hera to lead poor Io away.

Pleased at her shrewdness, Hera called for her servant, Argus, a giant with one hundred eyes. Argus hurried forward and Hera commanded him to guard the heifer. Io hung her head, certain she was doomed forever. A giant with a hundred eyes would always be watching and there would be no chance of escape.

SPACE NOTES

- The constellation Taurus shows the front of the Bull, emerging from water.

- Taurus is home to two star clusters, the Pleiades and the Hyades. The Hyades look like the letter "V" and is made up of about 200 stars that are 140 light-years away. All of the stars in the "V" are members of the Hyades except for the brightest star, the red giant Aldebaran, which is 60 light-years from Earth.

- The Pleiades (M45) represents the Seven Sisters in Greek mythology. This open star cluster is 415 light-years away. People have also described the Pleiades as symbolizing seven children, as well as a bunch of grapes.

- Remnants of a supernova called the Crab Nebula (M1) can be found in Taurus. This eighth magnitude shroud of gas surrounds a pulsar—a neutron star that emits energy in pulses as it rapidly spins on its axis.

- Each year around November 3, dust and rock from a comet called Encke causes the Taurid meteor shower. Under a dark sky, you might be able to spot about 10 meteors every hour.

Northern hemisphere: autumn

Southern hemisphere: spring

- One of the most distinctive constellations, Taurus is between Gemini and Aries. It is easily recognized as a bright letter "V" marked by the star Aldebaran, which is Arabic for "the follower" and represents the eye of the bull.

- You can locate Taurus by following a line up from Orion's belt. Another way to find Taurus is by starting at the bright stars in the neighboring constellation Gemini. Follow a line from Castor in Gemini to the red eye of the Bull. The Pleiades star cluster can also lead you to Taurus.

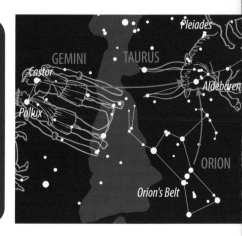

Watching from afar, Zeus saw the misery he had caused by allowing Hera to lead Io away. Realizing he could not save her without help, Zeus called upon his brother Hermes, the messenger god and god of luck. Well-known for his cunning, Hermes immediately came up with a plan to safely approach Argus.

Hermes sprang to the Earth dressed as a mortal. He carried a reed pipe and began to play a most pleasing tune as he purposefully wandered within sight of the giant. Already bored, Argus liked the music and asked Hermes to come closer and play for him. The messenger god sat next to the giant and played for the longest time, the shadows lengthening as the sun journeyed across the sky. Argus relaxed and some of his eyes closed in slumber. Yet some of his other eyes remained open.

Hermes frowned. He had hoped his music would lull the giant to sleep and that all one hundred eyes would be closed! Hermes began talking in a flat dull tone. He told Argus the most boring stories he could think of, droning on and on, until one by one, Argus's different eyes began to blink more slowly. At last all of the giant's eyes were closed. When Hermes was sure Argus was in a deep sleep, he drew his sword and killed the giant. Io was free.

Hera saw that Argus was slain and honored him by taking his eyes and placing them in the stars. They make the tail of Pavo, the Peacock, a southern hemisphere constellation.

Hera never liked to give up and sent a gadfly to follow the heifer wherever she wandered. Io tried to escape the gadfly's constant pestering by walking into the ocean. This ocean was later named the Ionian Sea, as well as the Bosphorus, a waterway meaning "the Ford of the Cow."

Io eventually fled to Egypt, where Zeus turned her back into a maiden. From that time on Io lived a life of happiness and privilege. Io and Zeus had a son named Epaphus, and one of Io's later descendants was the famous hero Hercules.

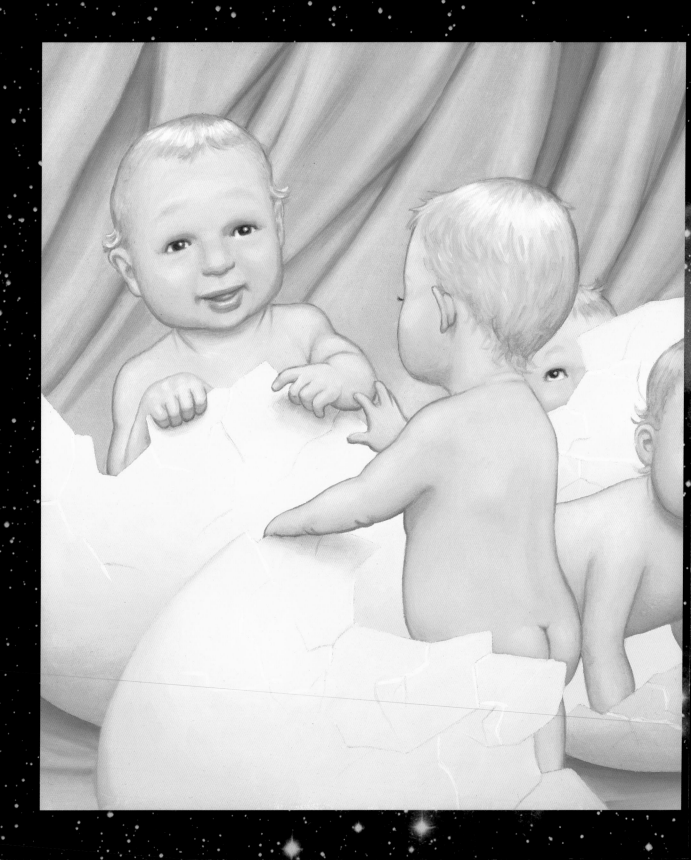

Gemini: The Twins
Third Sign of the Zodiac

Zeus, the king of the gods, had the ability to take any form or shape he wanted. One evening Zeus looked down from Mount Olympus and saw a maiden bathing in a lake. Overcome with romantic feelings, he disguised himself as a brilliant white swan and soared down to the water. Zeus splashed gently into the lake and swam up to the maiden, whose name was Leda. She was the Queen of Sparta, and was married to Tyndareus.

The elegant swan entranced Leda. She slowly reached out her hand, hoping to stroke its soft feathers. When the bird did not shy away, Leda was filled with delight. They began to play in the water, swimming alongside one another and splashing merrily. After some time, Zeus felt it was safe to reveal his true identity. He transformed back into his magnificent image as the king of the gods and shared a pleasant evening with Queen Leda.

Some time later Leda gave birth to four children by laying two eggs. Castor and Clytemnestra hatched from one egg. Their father was Tyndareus, so they were mortal. Pollux and Helen hatched from the other egg. Their father was the immortal god Zeus, so they would live forever.

Castor and Pollux grew up the closest of friends. Known as "the twins," they were also called "the Dioscuri," which means "sons of Zeus," even though Castor had a different father. Pollux was an incredible boxer and Castor was a talented horseman. The brothers became war heroes and enjoyed many adventures, including fighting with the Roman army as part of the cavalry and rescuing their sister Helen when another hero called Theseus tried to steal her away.

Sometimes the twins' adventures took place

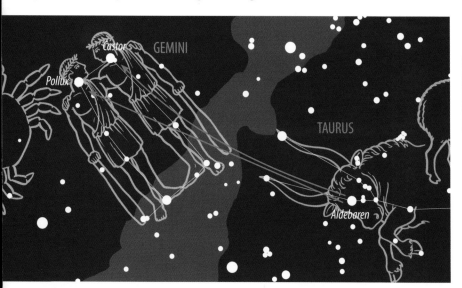

Find Gemini

Northern hemisphere: winter

Southern hemisphere: summer

- Gemini lies between Cancer and Taurus. Some of its stars are in the Milky Way, with the others extending east.

- You can locate Gemini by starting at Aldebaran, the red eye of the Bull in neighboring Taurus. Follow a line from Aldebaran to the stars Castor and Pollux.

SPACE NOTES

○ Yellow Pollux is the 17th brightest star in the sky and the most luminous star in Gemini. Castor is Gemini's second brightest star. Although it appears as a single star to the naked eye, Castor is actually a sextuple—three double stars!

○ Gemini contains an eighth magnitude planetary nebula officially named NGC 2392. Look at it through a telescope to see the odd shape that led to its common names—the Eskimo Nebula or Clown Face Nebula.

○ The Geminid meteor shower occurs every year when Earth passes through the dusty orbit of Asteroid #3200 Phaeton. Bits of asteroid dust burn up upon entering Earth's atmosphere, giving a show of shooting stars that appears to originate in Gemini. Check the sky from December 6-19. You can expect the most activity to occur from December 13-14. Most of the meteors seen in the Geminid shower are white, but some appear yellowish.

○ Two planets orbiting two different stars have been discovered in the constellation Gemini. HR 2877 is a giant star that is almost fifth magnitude. Its planet, estimated to be at least 6.5 times more massive than Jupiter, orbits HR 2877 every 303 days. The second planet orbits around the star HD 50554, a seventh magnitude dwarf star easily spotted with binoculars. This second planet has a mass at least 4.9 times the size of Jupiter and completes one orbit around HD 50554 every 3.5 years.

at sea. Castor and Pollux were famous for protecting sailors from pirates, as well as for calming violent storms. Legends claim that whenever the twins went on board a ship, two flames rose up its mast.

On one voyage the twins protected the crew of the Argo, a ship large enough to hold 50 men, called Argonauts. Jason, the leader of the Argonauts, welcomed heroes from all over Greece to join him on his quest to obtain the Golden Fleece—the pure gold pelt of a winged ram. The heroes sailed to the land of King Aeetes, where a dragon that never slept guarded the fleece. King Aeetes forced Jason to perform a number of dangerous tasks. Jason used great cunning to overcome each challenge and succeeded in taking the Golden Fleece from the dragon. Protected by the twins, Jason and his crew returned home with the Golden Fleece.

The twins' travels eventually brought them to the land of two Argonauts named Idas and Lynceus. When the twins argued with the Argonauts over some cattle, Idas became so enraged that he stabbed Castor, who died from his wounds.

Pollux was so forlorn over his brother's death that he begged Zeus to let him die too. He could not imagine life without Castor. Zeus could not grant his request because an immortal can never die. Instead he allowed Pollux to share his immortality with Castor and they were never separated again. The twins spend one day as deceased mortals in Hades, the underworld, and spend the next day as gods, on Mount Olympus. You can see Castor and Pollux reunited in the sky by Zeus. The two bright stars in Gemini represent the heads of the twins. The star Pollux follows the star Castor, setting in the west and rising in the east.

Cancer: The Crab
Fourth Sign of the Zodiac

Cancer the crab has a small part in Greek mythology. It appears briefly in a story about the hero Hercules, who was famous for his noble bravery and enormous strength. But as great as he was, Hercules was not a god and would not live forever. Although his father was Zeus, the king of the gods, his mother Alcmene was human and Hercules was half-mortal.

Wanting to become immortal and live forever, Hercules traveled to the town of Delphi to ask for advice from the oracle of Apollo. Skilled at foretelling the future, the oracle revealed that Hercules could solve his problem and become immortal by serving Eurystheus, who was the king of the ancient Greek city of Mycenae.

Hera, the queen of the gods, was jealous of Alcmene and did not like her son Hercules. She created trouble for the half-god whenever she could and urged Eurystheus to make him suffer. The king listened to Hera and commanded Hercules to overcome 12 difficult labors.

Hercules's second labor was to kill the terrifying Hydra, a monster that lived in a swamp near the city of Lerna in Greece. The Hydra was a nine-headed serpent with

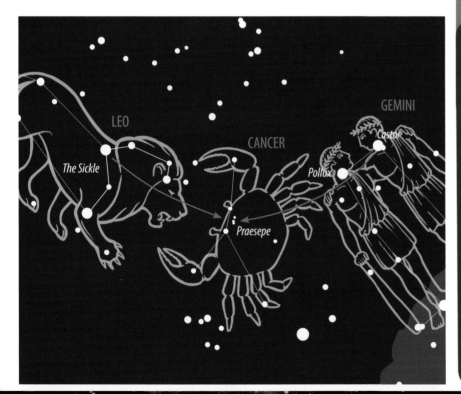

LEO

The Sickle

CANCER

Praesepe

GEMINI

Castor

Pollux

Find Cancer

Northern hemisphere: winter

Southern hemisphere: summer

- Cancer is the faintest constellation, but it is easy to find between the bright stars of Leo in the east and Gemini in the west.

- Look for Cancer on a moonless night by starting at Gemini. Jump from the bright stars Castor and Pollux to Cancer, just a bit south of Praesepe (M44), an open star cluster also known as the Beehive or Manger. You can also find Cancer from Leo. Make a line from the center of the Sickle asterism in Leo to Praesepe in Cancer.

poisonous blood. Its breath was so foul that anyone unlucky enough to breathe it in immediately dropped dead. For many years the Hydra terrorized all who passed near its home.

Hercules and his nephew Iolaus traveled to Lerna by chariot. They reached the swamp where the Hydra lived, climbed out of the chariot, and gathered sticks for a fire. When the fire burnt with a steady glow of orange flames, Hercules lit the tips of several arrows and said to Iolaus, "Stay with the horses while I find the serpent."

Hoping to draw the monster out of hiding, Hercules walked toward the shore of the swamp, firing flaming arrows into the water as he walked. The Hydra emerged from the swamp and eyed the hero with fury. Without warning, the Hydra charged Hercules, its nine heads hissing and snarling in rage. Hercules immediately drew his sword and held his breath to avoid the Hydra's foul stench. He deftly dodged the Hydra, then lunged forward and cut off one of its heads. Instantly two more ferocious snapping heads erupted in its place. The harder Hercules tried to overpower the beast, the more difficult the task became.

Hercules struggled to keep the Hydra back, desperately trying to think of a way to slay a beast that grew new heads every time one was sliced away. As he dodged back from the serpent to gasp for fresh air, Hercules glimpsed the blaze crackling from the fire and shouted to Iolaus, "Quick, bring a flaming stick!"

Iolaus seized a burning stick and bravely approached the Hydra. As soon as Iolaus was close enough, Hercules cut off one of its heads and shouted, "Put the stick to its

SPACE NOTES

- Cancer's brightest star is called Al Tarf, which means "the end" in Arabic. It has a magnitude of 3.5 and marks the tip of the crab's lowest leg.

- Cancer contains M44, an open star cluster called the Beehive because its stars look like a swarm of bees when seen through binoculars. You can see a faint patch of light with the naked eye, but binoculars or an amateur telescope will help you to distinguish about 60 of M44's approximately 700 stars. M44 is also called the Praesepe, which means "the Manger" in Latin.

- The first day of summer is marked by the summer solstice, which takes place on the day the Sun reaches its most northerly point in the sky. Today the summer solstice occurs in Gemini, but centuries ago it occurred in Cancer. The Tropic of Cancer, named after the crab, refers to the latitude 23.5 degrees north of the equator.

- Four planets are believed to orbit the double star system named 55 Cancri in Cancer. The star system's biggest planet is at least 4.1 times more massive than Jupiter and takes 14.7 years to complete one orbit around 55 Cancri. The other three planets are closer to the star system and less massive.

wound!" Iolaus reached forward and thrust the burning stick against the Hydra's neck. The cut sealed with a sizzling hiss and stopped more heads from growing.

At this point Hera looked down from Olympus and saw that the Hydra was in trouble. She tried to help the beast by sending Cancer, the giant crab, to attack Hercules. Cancer darted from side to side, snapping and biting at Hercules's feet, trying to make him fall. It was hard to tell what direction the crab would attack from next, but Hercules managed to dodge the giant creature again and again. Cancer did not give up so Hercules finally jumped into the air and landed on its back. He jumped up and down, crushing Cancer's shell with his feet, until the crab finally stopped moving. Just in time, Hercules turned back to the snarling Hydra.

Seven more times Hercules cut off one of the Hydra's heads and seven more times Iolaus sealed the wounds shut with the burning stick. At last only one head taunted them, but when Hercules struck it with his sword, the blade bounced off the Hydra. Its life could not be easily ended, for no weapon could hurt the last head.

Hercules refused to give up. Drawing upon his mighty strength, he grabbed the Hydra's neck and tore the last head from its body. At last the Hydra was dead. Hercules dug a deep hole, threw the head into it, and covered it with a large rock. Reaching for his arrows, Hercules dipped them in the Hydra's poisonous blood to make his weapons even more deadly.

Hercules had completed the second of his 12 labors. Because the crab lost his life doing her bidding, Hera placed it in the sky as the constellation Cancer.

SPACE NOTES

- Leo Minor is a small dim constellation above Leo.

- The ancient Babylonians described the stars of Leo as looking like a fierce guard dog. The Taulipang Indians of northern Brazil saw the constellation as Tauna, a god of thunder and lightning. The Chinese saw the Rain Dragon called Hien-youen in the Sickle of Leo, while the Chukchi Native people of Arctic Siberia saw a sleeping woman.

- The Leonid meteor shower occurs every November 15–20. Sometimes the Leonids display only a few meteors, while other times there is a spectacular show. You can usually expect to see about 15 meteors per hour. In 1833 more than 100,000 meteors per hour were seen. In 1966 more than 100 meteors per second were seen for short bursts of time. The Leonid meteor shower is fairly easy to see, but it is only intense every 33 years when the comet Tempel-Tuttle passes close to Earth.

Leo: The Lion
Fifth Sign of the Zodiac

Eurystheus, king of the city of Mycenae, told Hercules he must tackle 12 labors to become immortal. One of his tasks was to fight the gigantic Nemean lion. The lion had lived on the Moon before traveling to the Earth as a falling star and terrorizing everyone it saw. The king told Hercules that the fearsome lion was known to roam the Nemean forest in the land of Argolis.

Hercules immediately gathered his bow, arrows, and club and left to search for the lion's home. He reached the Nemean forest and entered on foot, scanning the ground for tracks or some other sign to show the lion might be nearby.

Hercules hoped to discover the lion's lair and searched each animal trail with no success until a tremendous roar startled him from behind. He spun around to see the angry lion hurtling straight toward him. Raising his bow, Hercules fired at the beast's chest. The arrow struck its mark but fell to the ground without slowing the massive animal a single pace. Hercules tried again, firing arrow after arrow as the creature bore down upon him. Each arrow fell away, its point bent, unable to penetrate the animal's thick skin.

Snarling wildly, the lion pounced upon Hercules with a mighty leap. Falling backwards, Hercules swung his club over his head and struck the beast with all his might. The stunned lion's eyes became glazed, but he did not stop clawing and biting Hercules.

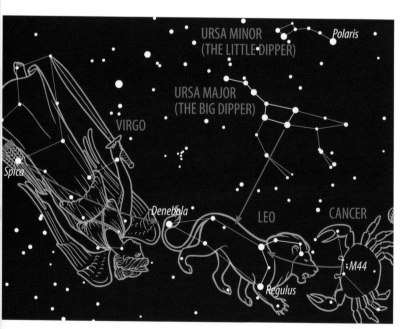

Find Leo

Northern hemisphere: spring

Southern hemisphere: autumn

- Leo is an easily recognized constellation between Virgo and Cancer. The Lion's head and forelegs are seen in an asterism called the Sickle, which looks like a backwards question mark. The star Regulus is the brightest star in Leo. The other bright star Denebola shows its tail.

- Look for Leo by making a line from Praesepe (M44) in Cancer to the Sickle in Leo. You can also reach Leo by starting at the bright star Spica in Virgo and leaping to Regulus in Leo. If you start at the Big Dipper, follow the pointer stars away from Polaris, the North Star, to reach the Lion.

Trying to twist away from the lion's snapping jaws, Hercules realized his weapons were not powerful enough to save him. He let the club fall to the ground and tackled the lion with his hands. Rolling and wrestling, Hercules managed to work his arms around the lion's shaggy neck. He pulled his arms tight, until unable to breathe, the lion slumped to the ground. Hercules pulled himself out from beneath the lion's body and looked down at the fearsome creature. It would make a fine trophy.

Anxious to return to Mycenae, Hercules removed his knife from its sheath so he could skin the lion. He tried to pierce the lion's skin but the hide was so tough that the knife only slid away. He tried to tear its skin with his bare hands, but even his mighty strength was not enough. Finally, Hercules took the beast's own sharp claws and used them to remove the head and pelt. The lion's head became Hercules's helmet and its hide became his cloak, now protecting him as it had once protected the wild beast.

Hercules returned to Mycenae dressed this way. When the king saw him approach, he immediately realized Hercules had completed the task. Eurystheus became frightened. He was certain that anyone who could kill the Nemean lion was dangerous and refused to let Hercules inside the city gates. The hero was forced to stay outside Mycenae and learn about the rest of his labors through the king's messenger. Zeus returned the Nemean lion to the heavens as the constellation Leo.

Knowing the Sky

Now you know how to find the 12 constellations of the zodiac. There are many more constellations to explore, as well as numerous other celestial wonders, from comets and meteors to Messier objects and distant galaxies. The more time you spend gazing at the heavens, the greater your observational skills will become. The night sky will become a familiar place, rich with stories about the gods, creatures, and heroes imagined by ancient cultures so very long ago.

Although astrology has no place in the true science of astronomy, it is fun to know your zodiac sign and look for your own constellation in the sky. Knowing you can find your way around the heavens is an incredible feeling. It gives you a sense of being connected with the vast universe—a frontier with so much yet to explore.

Amateur astronomers have made many interesting and significant discoveries. Perhaps you will be the next person to spot a new comet, locate an asteroid, or find something never seen before among the stars. Have fun starting your exploration by connecting the dots in the sky!

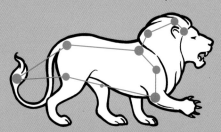

Glossary

apparent path the view we see of a celestial object's movement from our perspective on Earth.

Arabic language spoken by Arab people.

asterism a distinct pattern of stars that are part of one or more constellations.

asteroid a chunk of rock or metal in space, usually considered to be greater than one kilometer (0.6 mile) in diameter.

astrology the ancient belief that the positions of the stars, planets, Sun, and Moon influence your character and destiny.

astronomer a person who studies astronomy.

astronomy the science of studying celestial bodies, including their distance, brightness, size, motion, position, and composition.

atmosphere the gases that surround a celestial body, such as a planet.

axis an imaginary line through the center of a celestial object, around which the object turns. The ends of the axis are the north and south poles of the object.

Babylonians people who lived in the ancient city of Babylon, an area that is now in the country Iraq.

black hole a collapsed celestial object (either a former massive star or the massive core of a galaxy) whose gravity is so strong that nothing can escape, not even light.

brown dwarf see dwarf star.

celestial relating to the sky.

centaur a fabled creature that is half-man and half-horse, said to live in the mountains of Thessaly in Greece. A centaur is also a celestial object with the same characteristics as both comets and asteroids.

comet a celestial object of ice, rock, and dust that orbits the Sun. When comets pass near the Sun, they develop tails of gas and dust that point away from the Sun.

constellation a group of stars that represent an imaginary figure and belong to one of the 88 officially recognized star patterns, used to define different areas of the sky.

Cyclops mythical giants with a single eye in the middle of their foreheads.

deep sky objects celestial objects beyond the solar system, such as nebulae, star clusters, and galaxies.

degree a unit used to describe angular measurements in astronomy. There are 360 degrees in a circle.

diameter the length of a straight line passing through the center of an object, such as a sphere.

dwarf star a small star of average or below-average brightness. The Sun is a yellow dwarf. Brown dwarfs have masses between those of stars and the giant planets.

ecliptic the imaginary circle in the sky that marks the apparent annual path of the Sun against the background of stars. The apparent paths of the Moon and most of the planets are close to the ecliptic. The band of the zodiac extends eight degrees on either side of the ecliptic.

equator an imaginary circle around a planet or Moon that divides the north and south hemispheres, halfway between the north and south poles.

equinox the two times each year that the Sun crosses Earth's equator, making day and night of nearly equal length everywhere on Earth.

fireball a brilliant meteor.

galaxy a collection of billions of stars, gas, and dust, held together by gravity.

globular cluster a circular group of up to a million stars held together by gravity.

Gorgon one of three sisters in Greek mythology who were so ugly that anyone who looked at them turned to stone.

gravity the force that causes objects to fall or be pulled toward another object.

hemisphere any half of a celestial sphere.

horizon the place where the sky and Earth appear to meet.

horoscope a fanciful description of an individual's characteristics, personality, and future based on the positions of the nine planets and the stars in the zodiac at a specific time, such as at one's birth.

latitude the angular distance measured north or south of Earth's equator, or the angular distance of a celestial object from the ecliptic.

light pollution an inefficient use of light that illuminates areas other than those intended, such as the sky rather than the ground. The glare and excessive brightness can make it difficult to view faint celestial objects.

light-year the distance light travels in one year, equalling 9.46 trillion kilometers (5.88 trillion miles).

magnitude a measurement of the brightness of a celestial object. The dimmer the star is, the higher its magnitude. A first magnitude star is one hundred times brighter than a sixth magnitude star.

mass a measure of how much matter an object contains.

matter the material that a physical object is made up of.

Messier objects one of 110 deep sky objects identified and catalogued by Charles Messier to help people using small telescopes know these objects were not comets.

meteor a streak of light seen in the sky, caused by fragments of rocks and dust burning upon entering Earth's atmosphere. Meteors are also called falling stars or shooting stars.

meteor shower when a larger than normal number of meteors enter the atmosphere during a short period of time and appear to come from the same area of the sky.

Milky Way Galaxy the name of the galaxy where Earth is located, which appears as a band of light seen across the night sky. It is about one hundred thousand light-years across and contains some two hundred billion stars.

mortal unable to live forever.

myth a story involving imaginary characters that may be used to explain an event, practice, belief, or natural occurrence.

naked eye eyesight that is not assisted by binoculars or a telescope.

nebula a cloud of dust and gas within a galaxy, where new stars are formed, or the remains of a star whose life has ended in an explosion.

neutron star a very small dense star with intense gravity that remains after a supernova explosion. A neutron star has a diameter of about 40–60 kilometers (60–100 miles).

North Star the star almost directly above the North Pole. The axis of Earth's north geographic pole points at the North Star, which is currently Polaris.

northern hemisphere the half of Earth that is north of the equator.

open cluster see star cluster.

orbit the path of one celestial body around another.

planet a celestial object that is so massive, its own gravity has forced it into a spherical shape. Planets move in an orbit around a star. The different classes of planets include our Sun's four terrestrial planets (dense, rocky, and Earth-like) — Mercury, Venus, Earth, and Mars; four Jovian planets (low density, gaseous, and Jupiter-like) — Jupiter, Saturn, Uranus, and Neptune; and many small, ice-rich dwarf planets, including Pluto. Dwarf planets have masses that are too low to have any gravitational effect on other planets.

planetary nebulae bubble-shaped clouds of gas ejected from low-mass, dying stars.

precession the slow gyration, or wobble, of Earth's axis, caused by the gravitational attraction of the Sun and Moon.

protostar a star that is still forming from a cloud of dust and gas in space.

pulsar a neutron star that emits energy in pulses as it rapidly spins.

rotate to spin around an axis.

solar system The Sun and all the objects that orbit around it, including the planets, and more than 150 moons of the planets, as well as asteroids, comets, and meteoroids. Since the mid-1990s, planets have been discovered orbiting stars other than our Sun. These stars and their planets are called extra-solar systems or stellar planetary systems.

solstice either of the two points on the ecliptic where the Sun is at its greatest distance from the celestial equator, marking the first day of summer and the first day of winter.

southern hemisphere the half of Earth that is south of the equator.

star a hot sphere of glowing gas that emits energy and light. Our Sun is a star.

star cluster a group of stars close to each other in space and born at the same time, out of the same material. Open clusters are loose groups containing a few hundred stars. The stars in globular clusters are closer together and number in the thousands.

supergiant a very bright star and the largest known type of star.

supernova the explosion of a very massive star, resulting in a sharp increase in brightness followed by gradual fading.

Titan a member of the family of giants parented by Uranus and Gaia.

Zeus king of the gods in Greek mythology.

zodiac an imaginary band in the sky divided into 12 constellations, where the Sun, Moon, and planets appear to travel. The constellations, or signs, of the zodiac are Aries, Taurus, Gemini, Cancer, Leo, Virgo, Libra, Scorpius, Sagittarius, Capricornus, Aquarius, and Pisces.

Index

About the Author/Illustrator

Joan Marie Galat lives near Edmonton, Alberta, where she operates MoonDot Media, a communications business offering writing and editing solutions in broadcast, print, and multi-media. A frequent presenter on astronomy, writing, and creativity, Joan attended an international book festival in Seoul, where she gave presentations highlighting the Korean translations of Dot to Dot in the Sky.

Besides writing and astronomy, Joan's favorite activities include spending time outdoors, picnicking, walking, cycling, swimming, rollerblading, playing chess, and of course reading!

Joan has three children. She often visits schools, where she enjoys using storytelling to share her knowledge of the night sky with students of all ages. Her website at www.joangalat.com contains additional author information, astronomy links, and fun for kids.

Lorna studied Fine Arts at Grant MacEwan College and the University of Alberta. She has worked as a designer, writer, illustrator, and animator. Her illustrations in *Sandwiches for Duke* won her a nomination for the Amelia Frances Howard-Gibbon Award and *Dot to Dot in the Sky: Stories of the Moon* won an Alberta Book Award. Lorna currently devotes most of her time to children's educational and picture books, novel covers, greeting cards, technical illustration, and multimedia projects, as well as touring schools and libraries, teaching art, and working as a staff artist at the University of Alberta Hospital.

She especially loves mountain biking all year, skiing, hiking, photography, painting, foreign films, literature, music, cooking, and travelling. She lives in Edmonton, Alberta.